TOOTH TALES
from around the World

Marlene Targ Brill • Illustrated by **Katya Krenina**

Charlesbridge

A tooth is loose! What do you do? You jiggle it and wiggle it. You eat apples. You stand on your head. You string your tooth to a doorknob. You hold contests to see whose tooth twists the most.

Why? You want that tooth to come out.
You want the tooth fairy to come!

But the stubborn tooth hangs on, sometimes by just a thread. Until one day, you take a bite. Something hard rolls from side to side in your mouth, tasting salty from blood. You spit out a sharp lump.

It's your tooth! Now what do you do? Save it? Throw it away? Give it to someone for safekeeping?

For a long, long time, children around the world have followed special customs when they lose their teeth. Today, one popular custom is to leave each tooth for the tooth fairy. This good fairy sneaks into your room while you sleep and takes your tooth. You never hear or see a thing. But in the morning, you discover a surprise under your pillow—maybe a coin, a small present, or a snack sits where the tooth once was.

How does this treat get there? And who is the tooth fairy? No one knows for sure. But beliefs about lost baby teeth go back thousands of years, to a time when stories were passed by word of mouth, a time before anyone ever heard of the tooth fairy.

Almost five thousand years ago, some people in Asia and Africa thought teeth were a sign of strength. They saw that teeth and bones stayed as hard as stones long after a person died.

Ancient Egyptians believed that the sun helped make teeth even stronger. They threw lost teeth toward the sun saying: GIVE ME A BETTER ONE FOR IT.

Over the years, many groups have believed that everyone
has a spirit that lives on after people die. Some early
Europeans thought that these spirits could live forever
as long as their bodies were buried with
all of the parts, including the teeth.
To save baby teeth, mothers
put them in barrels, pockets,
or pots. They
returned
these teeth to
their children
when they grew up.

Other groups worried that evil spirits
might find their children's teeth. They
thought these spirits could use the teeth
to gain power over the children and
hurt them. Both bad spirits and
good spirits became known
as fairies and witches.

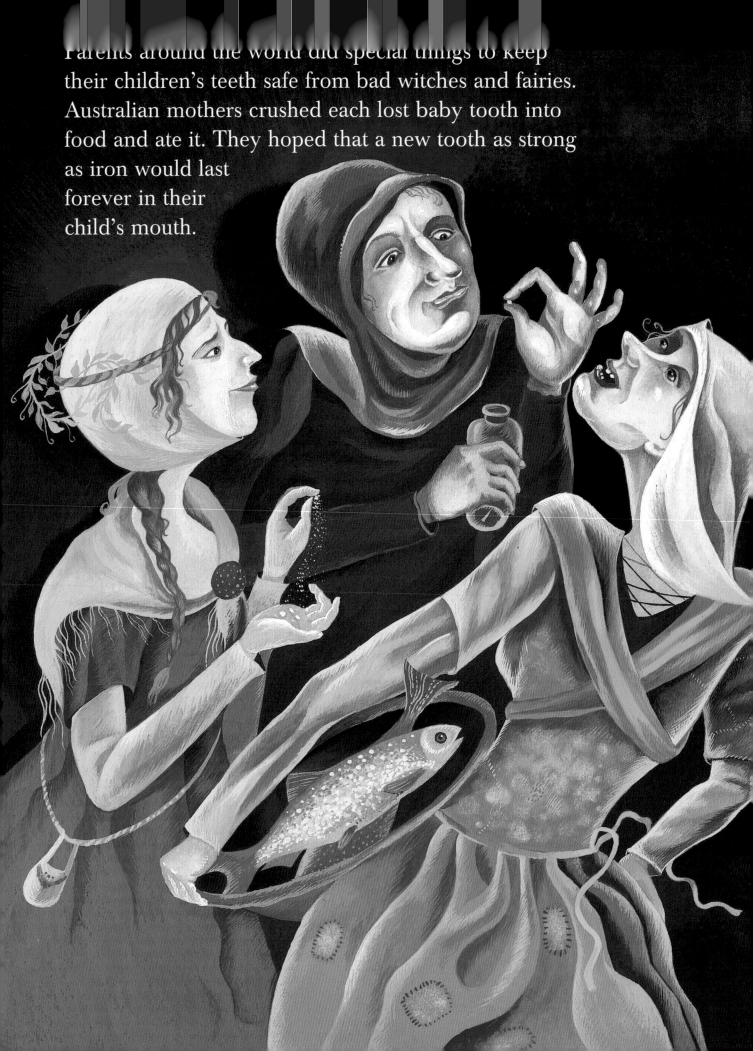

Parents around the world did special things to keep
their children's teeth safe from bad witches and fairies.
Australian mothers crushed each lost baby tooth into
food and ate it. They hoped that a new tooth as strong
as iron would last
forever in their
child's mouth.

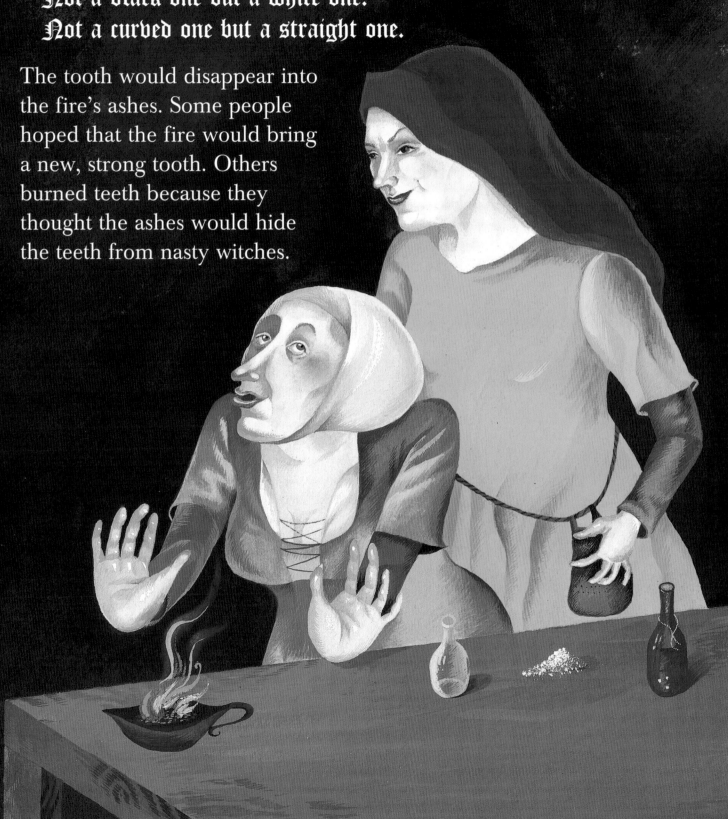

In parts of England, mothers put salt on the tooth to protect it. Then they burned it, while the children sang:

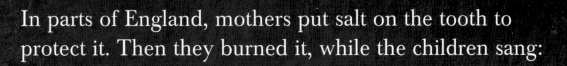

> Fire, burn; burn the tooth
> And give me another.
> Not a black one but a white one.
> Not a curved one but a straight one.

The tooth would disappear into the fire's ashes. Some people hoped that the fire would bring a new, strong tooth. Others burned teeth because they thought the ashes would hide the teeth from nasty witches.

Another way people kept teeth from evil witches was by giving them to animals. Witches were said to dislike certain animals, such as rats and snakes, so people thought teeth would be safe with them. Children hid their teeth near nests, under rocks, or behind fireplaces, anywhere rats and snakes might find them.

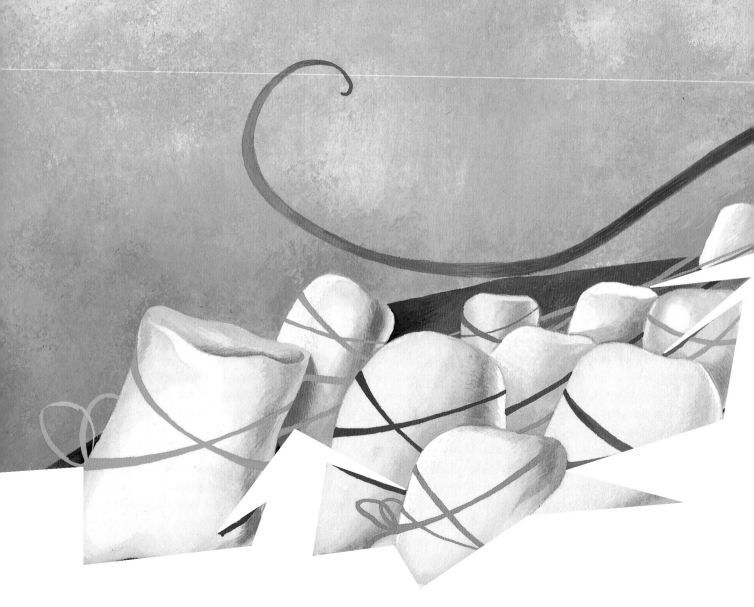

Ilocano children of the Philippines pulled out their teeth with string. Then they hid the teeth and the string in rat holes. The string was to help the rats drag the teeth away.

Over the years, the custom of giving teeth to animals took on new meaning. Boys and girls still offered baby teeth to them, but now they asked sharp-toothed animals—squirrels, cats, dogs, wolves, even hyenas—to bring them strong teeth in return.

Cherokee Indian children asked for beaver teeth. The children ran around their homes with their teeth. Then they threw the teeth on the roof, shouting:

Beaver put a new tooth in my jaw!

Beaver put a new tooth in my jaw!

Beaver put a new tooth in my jaw!

Beaver put a new tooth in my jaw!

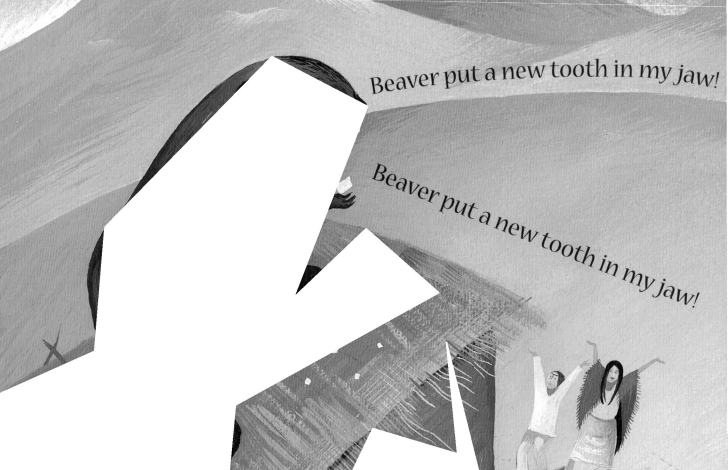

Other people did not like the idea of any animal finding a child's tooth. Until the late 1800s, parents in Canada and in parts of England and the eastern United States burned their children's teeth or hid them to keep them from animals.

They worried that a tooth just like the animal's would grow where the lost tooth had been. If a pig found their child's tooth, a pig's tooth might grow in its place!

In many cultures, the most popular creature of all was the tooth mouse. Children from Russia, New Guinea, and Egypt thought that mice could live through anything. They knew that mice had teeth that grew healthy and sharp, even after breaking. Some German and Armenian children believed mice were dead relatives who came back to life to help them grow strong teeth.

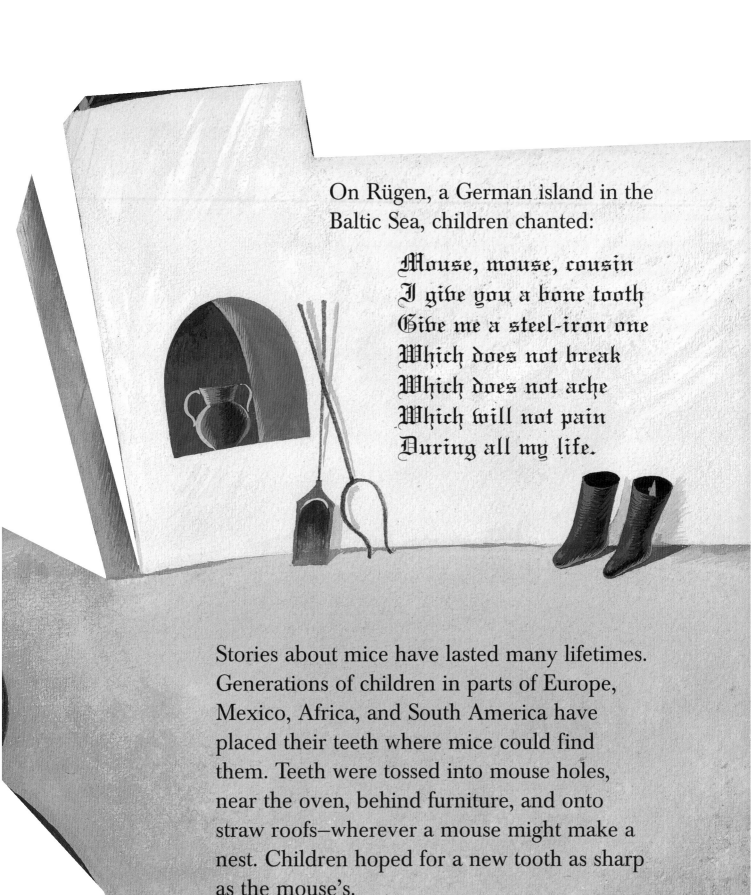

On Rügen, a German island in the
Baltic Sea, children chanted:

> Mouse, mouse, cousin
> I give you a bone tooth
> Give me a steel-iron one
> Which does not break
> Which does not ache
> Which will not pain
> During all my life.

Stories about mice have lasted many lifetimes.
Generations of children in parts of Europe,
Mexico, Africa, and South America have
placed their teeth where mice could find
them. Teeth were tossed into mouse holes,
near the oven, behind furniture, and onto
straw roofs—wherever a mouse might make a
nest. Children hoped for a new tooth as sharp
as the mouse's.

It was more than 100 years ago that children in Europe first began to receive treats from the tooth mouse. Sometimes, they found food. Other times, they found a coin or a small present. Everyone liked the idea of getting something in exchange for a lost tooth.

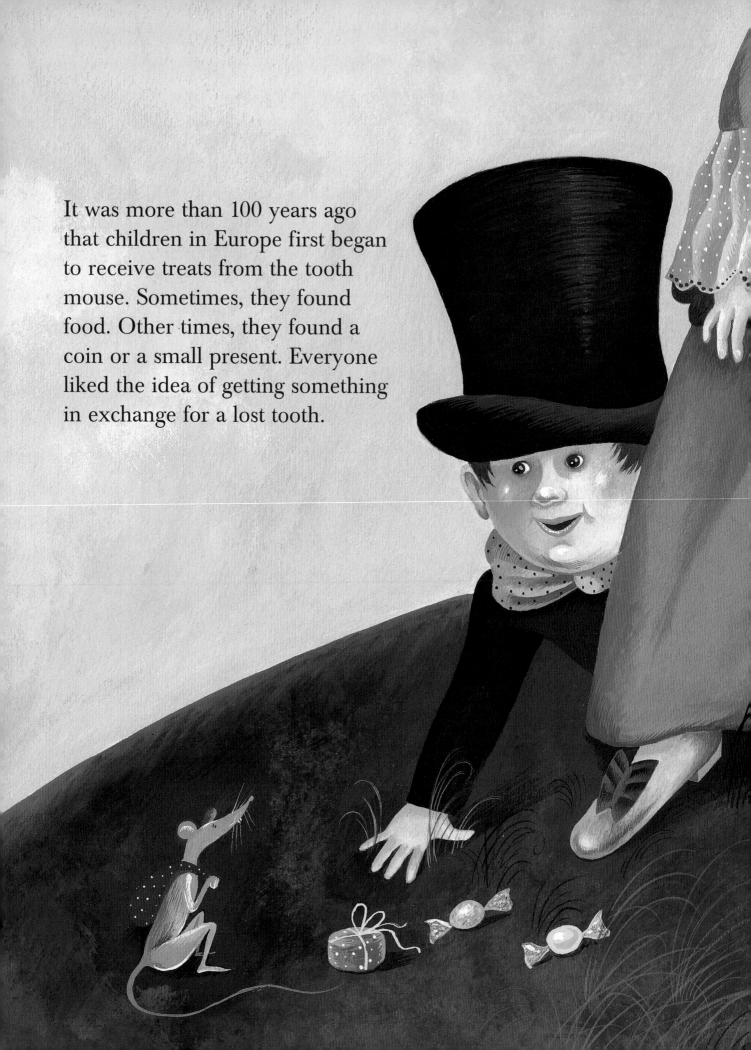

As time passed, a new legend began. People in the United States remembered their parents telling them about a good fairy who took away lost teeth. This fairy became known as the tooth fairy.

Since the 1940s, the belief in one fairy called the tooth fairy has also become popular in parts of Canada, Spain, and Great Britain. Children in families that follow the custom find treats from the tooth fairy whenever a baby tooth falls out. That's up to twenty tooth fairy visits for twenty baby teeth!

These children usually hide their lost tooth in secret places. Most often, they tuck it under a pillow at night. Some boys and girls hide their tooth in a glass of water, inside a slipper, or under the bed.

A few even have tooth pillows to keep their tooth from getting lost in the sheets, or they write letters asking to save the tooth for their collection. For all this work, the tooth fairy usually leaves a coin.

Today, children everywhere continue to follow different customs to mark losing their teeth. In countries such as Mexico and Poland, they still leave baby teeth in hiding places behind ovens and furniture. In return, they find small presents or snacks from the tooth mouse.

There are millions of other boys and girls around the world who have never heard of the tooth mouse. Their mothers have never eaten their teeth or thrown them into fires to keep them safe. They have never heard of evil witches or spirits that steal teeth. But when their teeth come out, these children are glad that they *have* heard of the tooth fairy.